THE ART OF SURRENDER

HOW LETTING GO ATTRACTS WHAT YOU TRULY DESIRE

SIMON BEDROS

Copyright © 2025 by Simon Bedros

Title: The Art of Surrender: How Letting Go Attracts What You Truly Desire

All rights reserved. No part of this publication may be copied, reproduced, stored in a retrieval system, or transmitted in any form or by any means—electronic, mechanical, photocopying, recording, or otherwise—without the prior written permission of the author, except for brief quotations used in reviews, articles, or educational materials.

This book is a work of original nonfiction. While the author has made every effort to ensure the accuracy and completeness of the information contained herein, it is not intended as a substitute for professional advice. The author disclaims any liability arising from the use or misuse of this material.

For requests to reproduce or adapt any part of this book, please contact the author directly.

CONTENTS

Preface   4

Introduction   7

1 *The "Let Go, Let God" Principle*	*12*
2 *When You Release, Life Responds*	*28*
3 *The Paradox Of Letting Go: Why Surrender Attracts Success*	*44*
4 *Releasing What Weighs You Down*	*62*
5 *The Flow State: What It Is And How To Achieve It*	*82*
6 *How To Make Affirmations Really Work To Manifest Your Dreams And Desires*	*99*
7 *Taking Action Without Attachment*	*118*

Conclusion And A Call To Action   136

Appendix: Practical Tools For Letting Go   142

Acknowledgments   198

About The Author   199

PREFACE

I've spent years helping people gain clarity, set goals, and envision the life they truly wanted.

And yet—time and time again—I witnessed something that troubled me.

Even those doing all the "right things" still felt stuck.

They had the vision. They took action. They believed.

But something deep inside was still holding on.

At first, I couldn't name it.

Was it fear? Resistance? Doubt?

Eventually, I realized it was something more subtle—and more powerful.

It was the inability to surrender.

Surrender doesn't mean giving up. It doesn't mean becoming passive or helpless.

In fact, true surrender is one of the most active, courageous things you can do.

It's the choice to let go of what you can't control so you can fully embrace what you can.

It's not a tactic.

It's not a mindset trick.

It's a way of being.

This book was born from that realization.

It's not about controlling life more—but about learning how to partner with it.

Not about resisting your pain—but about releasing what no longer serves you.

You don't need to be more perfect.

You don't need to prove yourself more.

You've already done enough striving.

Now it's time to let go.

If you've been gripping tightly to plans, people, outcomes, or old wounds, this book is your invitation to breathe again.

To stop carrying what was never yours to hold.

To stop running from what's asking to be felt.

To stop forcing what's meant to unfold.

Surrender isn't about giving up.

It's about returning—to trust, to peace, to yourself.

I don't offer this book as someone who's mastered surrender, but as someone who needed it—and found something beautiful on the other side.

PREFACE

If you're ready, I'll walk with you on the journey to mastering the art of surrender.

Let's begin.

INTRODUCTION

In a world that celebrates control, precision, and certainty, the concept of letting go seems almost heretical. We're taught to believe that holding on tight and managing every aspect of our lives is the key to success and happiness. But what if the opposite were true? What if the secret to achieving our desires lies in surrendering our need to control, embracing uncertainty, and allowing life to flow?

A PERSONAL MOMENT THAT CHANGED EVERYTHING

I still remember the night I truly understood the power of surrender.

At that time, I was facing one of the toughest decisions of my life—everything I had worked for seemed to be slipping through my fingers. I tried everything: planning harder, pushing harder, stressing over every detail. The more I fought, the worse things seemed to get.

Finally, exhausted and out of answers, I sat down, closed my eyes, and whispered: *"I let go. I trust what's meant for me will find me."*

It wasn't dramatic. It wasn't some grand gesture. It was quiet—a quiet decision to stop gripping so tightly and allow life to unfold.

Within days, an opportunity appeared—one I hadn't seen coming, better than anything I had been chasing. It felt as if life had been waiting for me to loosen my grip so it could step in and guide me toward something greater.

That night, I learned something I'll never forget:

Surrender isn't weakness. It's strength in its purest form.

And it's this quiet, powerful shift—the art of letting go—that this book is all about.

EXPLORING THE CONCEPT OF SURRENDER

Surrender is not about giving up or being passive. It's about releasing the heavy burden of trying to manage every detail and trusting that there's a greater force at work. It's akin to floating down a river instead of paddling upstream—while you still navigate the waters, you're no longer fighting against the current. This choice to "go with the flow" opens up a world of possibilities.

In many spiritual traditions, surrender is considered a gateway to deeper understanding and connection. The phrase "Let Go, Let God" captures this essence, suggesting that by relinquishing control, we invite divine guidance into our lives. This act of faith is not limited to religious contexts; it's about embracing a broader perspective and recognizing that we're part of something much larger than ourselves.

UNDERSTANDING THE BENEFITS OF LETTING GO

The benefits of letting go are profound. On a practical level, it reduces stress and anxiety. When we're constantly striving for control, we create tension within ourselves. Our minds are filled with worries about outcomes, and our bodies react to this stress. By choosing to let go, we give ourselves permission to breathe, relax, and trust in the journey.

Letting go also leads to a profound sense of freedom. It's like cleaning out a closet that's been packed with clutter for years. As you clear away the old, you make room for the new—new ideas, new opportunities, and new relationships. This process of decluttering can be both physical and metaphorical, allowing us to shed outdated beliefs, toxic connections, and unnecessary worries.

Moreover, when we let go, we often find that what we desire comes to us in unexpected ways. It's a paradox: by releasing our tight grip, we create the space for things to flow to us naturally. Consider the stories of people who found their perfect partner only after they stopped obsessively searching or those who discovered financial success when they let go of their fear of failure. These moments of serendipity are not mere coincidences; they are the result of surrendering to the flow of life.

LETTING GO AND THE JOURNEY AHEAD

As you delve into the chapters ahead, you'll explore personal stories and practical techniques that illustrate the transformative power of letting go. You'll learn how to find balance in taking action without becoming attached to outcomes, how to enter the state of flow where creativity and productivity thrive, and how to trust in the journey even when the path is unclear.

This book is an invitation to embrace surrender as a powerful tool for personal growth and success. It's a journey of exploration, where you'll discover that the art of letting go can lead to profound transformation. As you read on, consider this your guide to unlocking the hidden potential that lies within you, waiting to be set free by the simple act of letting go.

REFLECTION EXERCISE:

Take five minutes right now to reflect and write down three specific areas in your life where you're currently trying to control outcomes. Next to each, write a brief statement about how surrendering control might positively impact your stress levels, relationships, or overall happiness. Keep these reflections in mind as you read further and begin practicing the art of surrender.

Now that we've set the stage and opened ourselves to the possibility that letting go might be our greatest source of power, it's time to explore a foundational principle that brings this idea to life. In Chapter 1, I'll dive into the timeless wisdom of the "Let Go, Let God" principle—an idea that has guided countless individuals toward peace, clarity, and meaningful success. Together, we'll uncover how this simple yet profound mindset can transform your daily experiences, offering both practical strategies and deep insights for releasing control and embracing the natural flow of life.

1

THE "LET GO, LET GOD" PRINCIPLE

"Let Go, Let God"—a phrase embodying freedom and relief, suggesting that by releasing control, we find peace and invite good things into our lives. Rooted deeply in faith and trust, this principle extends beyond spirituality and resonates universally with anyone seeking relief from the pressures of modern life. When we stop trying to force outcomes, we create space for life to unfold naturally, often in beautiful and unexpected ways.

ORIGINS AND INTERPRETATION

"Let Go, Let God" originates from religious teachings, especially within Christianity, urging believers to trust in God's plan. Its simplicity holds profound implications: releasing the desire to control everything allows us to align with a greater purpose and harmony with life's natural order.

Yet, this principle transcends religious boundaries. Broadly interpreted, it encourages us to release anxiety and stress by accepting that we can't—and don't need to—control every detail. At its core, it invites us to adopt a mindset of openness, freeing us from the exhausting cycle of micromanaging our existence.

APPLYING THE PRINCIPLE TO EVERYDAY LIFE

Implementing "Let Go, Let God" transforms our daily experiences by shifting our focus away from uncontrollable factors to the choices we can genuinely influence—our reactions and perspectives. Consider moments of everyday stress, such as traffic delays or unexpected schedule changes. Stressing over these won't alter the outcomes, but letting go of the tension can transform your day.

This principle encourages balanced ambition. You can set clear goals and take purposeful action without becoming fixated on specific outcomes. By remaining open to alternative paths, you may discover unexpected opportunities that surpass your original intentions.

A PERSONAL EXAMPLE: TRUSTING WHEN I WANTED TO FORCE

Years ago, I faced a situation where everything in me wanted to force an outcome.

THE "LET GO, LET GOD" PRINCIPLE

I had been working tirelessly toward a project I deeply cared about. I mapped every detail, envisioned every step, and pushed harder with every setback. Yet no matter what I did, doors kept closing. Meetings fell apart. Opportunities that seemed certain dissolved overnight.

Frustration built until it felt unbearable. I was ready to double down even harder—to strategize more, to push more, to try and *make* it happen.

But in a moment of quiet exhaustion, I remembered the very principle I had studied but rarely lived fully: *"Let Go, Let God."*

I made a choice—not just intellectually, but emotionally.

I sat down, closed my eyes, and whispered:

> *"If this is meant for me, it will come. If not, I trust there's something better."*

I didn't know what would happen next. I just knew I couldn't keep living in that tight, anxious state.

Within weeks, something unexpected appeared: an opportunity I hadn't even considered—one that turned out to be far more aligned with my values, my energy, and my long-term purpose. It wasn't what I had planned, but it was exactly what I needed.

That experience taught me something I now carry into every area of my life:

Surrender doesn't mean losing. It means making space for something better to find you.

This is the real power of "Let Go, Let God" — not giving up, but giving over. Trusting that life, God, or the universe can work in ways we can't always see.

PRACTICAL EXERCISES TO APPLY "LET GO, LET GOD"

If you're ready to practice letting go in your own life, here are some simple, powerful tools you can start using today:

Daily Let-Go Journal:

Each evening, reflect briefly and write down one stressful moment from your day.

Next to it, write down how you could've surrendered control in that moment, and how this shift might have improved your experience.

Mindfulness Pause:

When facing stressful situations, practice a quick mindfulness pause:

Close your eyes, take three deep breaths, and silently say, "I Let Go, I Let God."

Feel the tension release with each exhale.

Weekly Reflection:

Every weekend, review your journal entries. Identify patterns where you're struggling to surrender control.

Set a simple intention for the coming week to consciously apply the "Let Go, Let God" principle in those areas.

Practice Gratitude:

At the end of each day, list three things you're grateful for—especially noticing areas where letting go allowed something positive to unfold naturally.

By consistently incorporating these practices, you'll start cultivating a mindset of trust and openness.

Embracing "Let Go, Let God" isn't about passive resignation—it's about active trust. It's a way of living that invites peace, possibility, and profound transformation.

REFLECTION EXERCISE

Take a moment now to identify one area in your life where you feel excessive control is causing tension or unhappiness.

Write down a brief commitment to practice the "Let Go, Let God" mindset in this area for the next seven days.

Notice how this changes your experiences and emotions.

Having explored the transformative power of the "Let Go, Let God" principle, we now understand how embracing surrender can profoundly impact our spiritual and emotional well-being. But how does this principle play out in the tangible, everyday moments of our lives?

In the next chapter, I step into a quiet moment—one that seemed insignificant at first, yet revealed everything.

What began as a simple act of sorting through the past became a mirror, reflecting who I was no longer… and who I was becoming.

Because sometimes, surrender doesn't arrive as a grand decision.

It starts with the smallest release—

A drawer cleaned, a memory let go, a truth finally faced.

These small acts prepare us.

They build the strength to let go when life later asks us to release something far greater.

NOTES

NOTES

NOTES

NOTES

NOTES

NOTES

NOTES

NOTES

NOTES

NOTES

2

WHEN YOU RELEASE, LIFE RESPONDS

Clothes often serve as a visual record of our lives, holding memories and reflecting our evolving sense of self. But what happens when the clothes you once loved suddenly don't fit or feel right anymore?

One spring, I opened my closet expecting to welcome back old favorites, only to find that many items no longer suited me. Shirts felt uncomfortably tight, jeans that had once been staples now felt awkward, and jackets seemed completely out of style.

At first, it was disheartening. These clothes weren't just fabric—they held memories of backyard barbecues, adventures, laughter, and seasons of life I once cherished. Letting go felt like losing pieces of who I had been.

But standing there, it became clear:

I had changed. My needs, my values, even my body—everything had evolved.

Holding onto clothes that no longer fit was like holding onto outdated versions of myself. It was time to clear space—not just in my closet, but in my life.

Piece by piece, I let them go. Each item I placed in the donation pile felt like lifting a small weight off my shoulders.

And with every empty hanger, I noticed something powerful:

Space for new growth.

Space for a new version of me.

It was a small but profound act of surrender.

SMALL SURRENDERS PREPARE YOU FOR BIG ONES

What I didn't realize then was that this small act of clearing space was preparing me for something much bigger.

Sometimes life starts by asking you to release the easy things—the clothes, the outdated memories, the old versions of yourself—before it asks you to release what feels impossible to let go of: your expectations, your plans, your pride, even your survival instincts.

A few years later, I would face a moment that made cleaning out a closet seem laughably easy in comparison.

A BIGGER LESSON IN LETTING GO

There came a time when everything felt like it was falling apart—professionally, financially, emotionally.

Projects that once seemed certain collapsed. Financial pressure mounted. No matter how much I strategized, pushed, and fought, it felt like life was slipping through my fingers faster with every effort.

I remember one night sitting alone, completely drained.

Staring at endless plans, spreadsheets, to-do lists—none of which were producing the results I needed.

Fear gripped my chest.

Pride screamed at me to fight harder.

But somewhere deeper inside, a quieter voice said:

"Let it go."

I realized I was gripping so tightly to my expectations, my timeline, my version of "how things had to be" — that I was suffocating any room for life to surprise me.

That night, I closed my eyes, placed my hand over my heart, and whispered to the universe:

"I'm willing to lose it all if that's what needs to happen.

I'm willing to be humbled.

I trust something greater is at work."

It wasn't resignation—it was full surrender.

I wasn't bargaining. I wasn't asking for a rescue.

I was finally, deeply trusting.

And then something incredible happened.

Within 48 hours, an unexpected opportunity appeared—a door I hadn't even known existed.

Not only did I avoid going under financially, but I also pivoted into work that aligned far more with who I truly was.

Looking back, I realize:

If I had clung harder to the old plans, I would have missed the miracle life was trying to hand me.

Surrender didn't break me.

It saved me.

WHY LETTING GO MATTERS

Letting go isn't about losing.

It's about trusting that life sometimes has better plans than the ones we're stubbornly clinging to.

Just like clearing out a closet creates space for clothes that actually fit, clearing out emotional attachments creates space for a life that fits who you are now—not who you used to be.

Surrender is not weakness.

It's wisdom.

PRACTICAL EXERCISE: YOUR OWN WARDROBE OF LESSONS

If you're ready to experience the transformative power of letting go in a tangible way, here's a simple practice you can try:

- Set aside 30–60 minutes this week to revisit your closet or personal belongings.
- Try on or hold each item and ask yourself honestly:
  * "Does this fit the person I am today—or the person I'm becoming?"
  * "Am I keeping this out of love—or out of fear?"
- Make three piles:
  * Keep: Items aligned with who you are now.
  * Donate: Items that no longer serve you, but could bless someone else.
  * Discard: Items past their usefulness.
- As you release each item, say silently: *"I let go of what no longer serves me.*

  I create space for new growth."

REFLECTION EXERCISE: JOURNAL YOUR EXPERIENCE

After your clear-out, spend 10 minutes reflecting on these questions:

- What emotions surfaced as you let go?
- What memories or attachments were hardest to release?
- What did this teach you about who you are becoming?

Now that we've seen how surrender—whether small or massive—creates freedom and space for growth, we're ready to explore something even deeper.

In the next chapter, **The Paradox of Letting Go: Why Surrender Attracts Success**, I'll uncover how releasing your grip on outcomes doesn't push your dreams away—it invites them in.

NOTES

NOTES

NOTES

NOTES

NOTES

NOTES

NOTES

NOTES

NOTES

NOTES

3

THE PARADOX OF LETTING GO: WHY SURRENDER ATTRACTS SUCCESS

Surrender is a principle that shows up in some of the oldest, most powerful teachings known to humanity.

In the Bible, the idea is woven throughout:

> *"Commit your way to the Lord; trust in Him, and He will act."* **(Psalm 37:5)**

The message is clear — release your need to control every outcome, and trust that something greater will unfold.

This truth isn't just found in spiritual teachings.

If you look closely, many of the world's most successful people intuitively understand the paradox:

- **Oprah Winfrey** has spoken often about how her greatest breakthroughs came only after she surrendered her obsessive chasing and said, *"I will let go. I will trust."*

- **Michael Jordan**, known for his legendary competitive spirit, often spoke about "letting the game come to him" rather than forcing every shot.
- **Steve Jobs** famously trusted the dots would connect even when he couldn't see the full path — a kind of surrender to intuition and timing.

Across all these examples, one pattern emerges:

When we stop grasping and controlling, life moves more easily in our favor.

WHY SURRENDER ATTRACTS SUCCESS

In a culture that emphasizes constant effort, achievement, and relentless pursuit, the idea of "letting go" might seem counterintuitive—even risky.

Yet, paradoxically, the act of surrendering creates space for success to flow in naturally.

Imagine trying to catch a butterfly with your hands.

The tighter and more frantic you get, the more it slips away.

But when you relax and sit still, the butterfly might just land on you.

Life works the same way.

Letting go doesn't mean abandoning dreams or giving up ambition.

It means **releasing your obsession with how and when things must happen**, so you're open to new possibilities—some of which may be better than anything you originally planned.

TWO REAL-LIFE STORIES OF SURRENDER

These two stories have stayed with me because they so clearly illustrate this paradox.

ALEX'S STORY:
LETTING GO TO FIND LOVE

I met Alex at a small gathering a few years ago, during a time when I was already deeply exploring the ideas of surrender and trust.

As we talked, Alex shared his journey.

He had spent years desperately searching for the perfect partner.

Dating apps, endless first dates, analyzing every message and gesture—it became a second job.

And the more he chased, the more elusive love seemed to become.

Finally, drained and discouraged, Alex decided to stop trying so hard.

He deleted the apps. He stopped searching.

Instead, he focused on himself: reconnecting with old friends, traveling, learning new skills, and simply living.

And then — without warning — love found him.

In the most ordinary of moments, while attending a friend's birthday party he almost skipped, Alex met the woman who would later become his wife.

When he let go, life brought him exactly what he was seeking all along.

SOFIA'S STORY: LETTING GO TO RISE HIGHER

Sofia's story came to me through a friend who worked with her.

She had been fiercely ambitious, always aiming for the next promotion, the next title, the next big win.

She worked overtime, volunteered for every project, chased recognition relentlessly.

Yet despite all her efforts, advancement kept slipping through her fingers.

At her breaking point, Sofia made a radical decision.

Instead of pushing harder, she decided to simply do her work with excellence — but detached from the need for immediate rewards.

She focused on mentoring others, deepening her skills, and enjoying the process.

Within months, leadership noticed the shift in her energy.

An unexpected promotion followed—one she hadn't even lobbied for.

Her surrender didn't guarantee a promotion. But it gave her something far more valuable first: peace. And from that peace, everything else began to change.

WHY THESE STORIES MATTER

What struck me about both Alex and Sofia was not just that good things eventually happened — but **how quickly doors opened once they truly let go**.

They didn't surrender as a strategy to manipulate life into giving them what they wanted.

They surrendered because they realized chasing wasn't working — and that trusting the process might be their only way forward.

And in that space of trust, **life responded**.

PRACTICAL EXERCISE: THE SURRENDER EXPERIMENT

If you want to experience this paradox for yourself, here's a simple challenge:

- Choose one specific area of your life—relationships, career, finances—where you notice yourself tightly holding onto an outcome.
- Clearly define the outcome you've been clinging to.
- For one week, consciously practice surrender.

Every time you catch yourself worrying or obsessing, pause and affirm:

> *"I trust the process. I release the need to control this outcome."*

- Shift your focus onto enjoying the process, not forcing the result.

REFLECTION QUESTIONS: DOCUMENT YOUR JOURNEY

At the end of the week, take some time to reflect — whether it's five minutes or an hour, whatever feels right for you.

- How did you feel while releasing control?

- What unexpected opportunities, moments, or insights appeared?
- Did you notice any changes in your emotional or physical well-being?
- What lessons did you learn about trust, openness, and flow?

DAILY AFFIRMATION

> *"By letting go, I create space for opportunities greater than I have imagined."*
>
> Say it each morning and watch how your energy—and life—begin to shift.

CLOSING THOUGHT

When we loosen our grip, something powerful happens:

Peace returns.

Creativity awakens.

And success often comes faster than when we were frantically chasing it.

Surrender isn't giving up.

It's opening up.

And while surrendering control can change your outer world, the real transformation begins within.

Yet, even when we mentally "let go," there's often hidden emotional weight we still carry—anger, grief, regret—that silently sabotages our progress.

In the next chapter, I'll dive deeper.

I'll explore how to recognize, face, and finally release the hidden emotional burdens that block our peace and success.

Because if surrender is the doorway, emotional release is the key.

Get ready to unlock it.

NOTES

NOTES

NOTES

NOTES

NOTES

NOTES

NOTES

NOTES

NOTES

NOTES

4

RELEASING WHAT WEIGHS YOU DOWN

> *"You will find that it is necessary to let things go; simply for the reason that they are heavy."*
> — C. JoyBell C.

Letting go sounds beautiful in theory.

But in practice, it often means confronting the emotions we've buried deepest—the ones that feel hardest to face.

This chapter isn't about pretending things are fine when they aren't.

It's about courageously feeling what's necessary to finally experience true emotional freedom.

Surrender isn't passive; it's the active choice to set down burdens you've carried for too long.

IDENTIFYING YOUR EMOTIONAL BACKLOG

We've all been hurt.

We've all experienced loss and disappointment.

Some of us have faced deep betrayal or grief—and kept moving forward, not because we fully healed, but because life didn't leave us a choice.

Here's the uncomfortable truth:

Unprocessed emotions don't vanish. They fester.

They disguise themselves as anxiety, anger, perfectionism, procrastination, or chronic fatigue.

If you feel stuck or blocked from achieving peace or success, chances are you're carrying emotional weight you no longer need.

THE INVISIBLE WEIGHT OF REGRET, FEAR, AND TRAUMA

Emotional burdens don't always show up as obvious pain.

- Sometimes they show up as regret — the haunting replay of what you could have done differently.
- Sometimes they appear as fear — paralyzing projections of everything that could go wrong.

- And sometimes, they manifest as the lasting shadows of trauma — moments you didn't choose, but that left deep imprints on your heart.

These invisible burdens are often the heaviest because they operate beneath the surface.

They quietly influence your thoughts, relationships, and decisions—without you even realizing it.

But here's the empowering truth:

No matter how long you've carried something, it's not too late to set it down.

You don't need to fix the past—you simply need to loosen your grip on it.

WHAT'S REALLY BEHIND THESE EMOTIONS

Let's unpack three common emotional burdens and what they usually signify:

- **Anger** often masks deeper pain or injustice. It emerges when we feel our boundaries or values have been violated.
- **Grief** is the emotional evidence of love lost. It's not limited to losing loved ones — it can also stem from unfulfilled dreams or unmet expectations.

- **Resentment** is recycled emotional pain. We replay old hurts hoping the person responsible will feel our pain. But ultimately, it's us who suffer the most.

Ironically, holding onto these emotions can feel like self-protection.

But in reality, it traps us in the past—keeping us energetically tethered to pain, fear, and limitation.

IF YOU WERE THE ONE WHO CAUSED HARM

Sometimes the pain we carry doesn't come from what was done *to* us — but from what we've done to others.

If you've hurt someone, knowingly or unknowingly, surrender still applies. But in this case, surrender begins with accountability.

You don't need to live in endless guilt to prove you've changed. But you *do* need to face the truth with humility. If possible, offer a sincere apology. Make amends where you can.

And then — let go.

Let go of the shame. Let go of the punishment you've been silently inflicting on yourself. Let go of the idea that you're unworthy of healing or growth.

Surrender doesn't mean forgetting. It means choosing to move forward with honesty, integrity, and compassion — not just for others, but for yourself.

THE REAL WORK: HOW TO LET GO

Letting go is more than a mindset — it's a **practice**.

Here's a four-step process designed not just to ease stress, but to help you release deeply anchored emotions that quietly shape your reality.

Step 1: Acknowledge What You're Feeling

Don't bypass your pain with positive thinking. Denial only buries the energy deeper.

Be radically honest:

- "I feel angry about what happened."
- "I feel grief about what I lost."
- "I feel fear about what might happen."
- "I feel resentment about what they did."

By acknowledging the emotion without judgment, you bring it out of the basement of your body and into the light of awareness.

Step 2: Welcome the Emotion Without Resistance

This step may feel counterintuitive — but it's powerful.

Welcome the feeling.

Don't fight it.

Don't rush to fix it.

Silently affirm:

"I accept this emotion. I don't need to change it right now. I just need to feel it."

When you stop resisting what is, your nervous system softens.

You move into a space of allowance—and allowance is the beginning of healing.

Step 3: Let the Energy Move

Now that the emotion has surfaced, let it move through you.

Healing isn't intellectual—it's physical, energetic, emotional.

Here are body-based release techniques:

- **TFT (Thought Field Therapy / Tapping)**

While focusing on a painful memory, gently tap meridian points on your face and chest.

It helps neutralize the emotional charge stored in your system.

- **The Sedona Method**

Ask yourself:

- "Could I let this go?"
- "Would I?"
- "When?"

Sit in these questions and notice what shifts inside you without forcing anything.

- **Breath Release**
  - Inhale deeply through your nose, focusing just below your belly button.
  - Exhale through your mouth, saying:

"I release and let go."

Repeat three times.

Visualize tension leaving your body with every breath.

- **Somatic (Body-Based) Release**

Emotions often lodge in the body.

Use gentle stretching, massage, foam rolling, shaking, or intuitive movement to unlock trapped feelings.

(If you've ever cried during a massage—you've felt this.)

Healing doesn't just happen in the mind.

It happens in the tissue, in the breath, and in the stillness.

> **Full step-by-step instructions and breakdowns of these techniques—including tapping points, movement examples, and guided prompts—can be found in the Appendix on page 142 at the end of the book.**
>
> Feel free to flip ahead if you want to dive deeper into any of them right now.

Step 4: Offer Forgiveness — For Your Freedom

Forgiveness isn't about excusing what happened.

It's about choosing not to carry the pain anymore.

You can say:

"I forgive [name/situation] because I choose peace and freedom for myself. This no longer defines me."

Forgiveness isn't weakness.

It's the ultimate act of reclaiming your power.

REFLECTION ACTIVITY: EMOTIONAL FREEDOM JOURNAL

Spend 10–15 minutes reflecting on:

- Which emotion (anger, grief, resentment, regret, fear) was hardest for me to face?
- What changed when I welcomed it instead of resisting?
- What technique helped me release it most effectively?
- What new story about myself can replace the old one I was carrying?

BONUS PRACTICE: HEART-CENTERED RELEASE VISUALIZATION

At night, place your attention on the center of your chest.

Visualize a glowing white ball of light — full of compassion and peace — expanding with each breath.

Imagine your anger, fear, or grief dissolving into this light.

Softly repeat:

"I release and let go.

I release and let go.

I release and let go."

Let it become your nightly ritual—an energetic cleansing before you sleep.

DAILY EMOTIONAL RELEASE CHECKLIST

Use this short checklist at night:

- Did I acknowledge what I felt today?
- Did I allow myself to feel it without resistance?
- Did I practice a form of emotional release?
- Did I rewrite the story or offer forgiveness?

Small consistent emotional releases lead to massive inner freedom.

DAILY AFFIRMATION

> *"I willingly release all emotions that no longer serve me.*
>
> *By letting go, I reclaim my joy, peace, and emotional freedom."*

CLOSING THOUGHT:

As you continue to release emotional weight, something remarkable happens:

- Peace returns.
- Clarity sharpens.
- You feel lighter.
- Life flows easier.

You naturally begin entering the **flow state** — where creativity, fulfillment, and happiness arise without force.

In the next chapter, **The Flow State: What It Is and How to Achieve It**, you'll discover how letting go becomes your personal gateway to high performance, deep presence, and effortless joy.

NOTES

NOTES

NOTES

NOTES

NOTES

NOTES

NOTES

NOTES

NOTES

NOTES

5

THE FLOW STATE: WHAT IT IS AND HOW TO ACHIEVE IT

Have you ever been so absorbed in something that you forgot to eat?

Or stayed up all night working on a project, not because you had to—but because you couldn't pull yourself away?

That's the flow state.

In flow, time bends.

Focus sharpens.

Creativity feels effortless.

In this chapter, we'll explore how to find your flow, what it unlocks in your life, and how to step into it more often.

UNDERSTANDING FLOW IN BUSINESS AND LIFE

Flow isn't just about being productive—it's about experiencing life at its most vibrant.

Psychologist Mihaly Csikszentmihalyi described flow as a state of complete immersion where you're so engaged, the world around you disappears.

It's the moment the music carries you away, or when a conversation sparks so much energy you lose track of time.

In business, flow is your secret weapon.

It's where innovation, focus, and true creativity ignite.

Outside of work, flow is why hobbies, passion projects, or even workouts can leave you feeling more alive than ever.

Flow isn't rare.

It's natural.

But you have to create the right conditions for it to show up.

A TRUE STORY OF FLOW: MICHAEL JORDAN'S ZONE

When you think of flow embodied, few names shine brighter than **Michael Jordan**.

Jordan wasn't just talented.

He lived in the zone.

When in flow, it was as if time slowed around him.

In games where everything was on the line, Jordan didn't tighten up or overthink. He moved with a grace that seemed supernatural—shooting with ease, reacting instinctively, anticipating the court before others even saw it.

But here's what most people miss:

Jordan didn't create flow through raw force.

He created it through presence.

He talked often about his mindset during those legendary games.

He wasn't worrying about the last shot he missed.

He wasn't anxious about what would happen if he lost.

He was simply there—in the moment—responding intuitively to what was in front of him.

"I never looked at the consequences of missing a big shot...

when you think about the consequences you always think of a negative result."

Jordan teaches us something profound about flow:

You can't be in the future and be in flow.

You can't be in the past and be in flow.

You have to be fully here.

When you surrender outcomes, stay rooted in presence, and allow your instincts to take over—that's when you enter your zone.

And whether you're building a business, writing a novel, cooking a meal, or having a conversation, that same zone is available to you.

HOW TENSION BLOCKS FLOW: RELEASING THROUGH THE BODY

Most people try to find flow through pure mental effort.

But what often goes unnoticed is the role your body plays.

Stress, grief, regret—they don't just live in your mind.

They lodge themselves in your shoulders, your chest, your gut.

When your body is tense, you're not in creation mode—you're in survival mode.

That's why **physical release is a gateway to flow.**

Before beginning a creative session or an important project, take a few minutes to prepare your body:

- **Stretch gently**—especially your neck, shoulders, and hips where tension hides.
- **Breathe deeply into your belly**, two inches below your navel. Slow, grounded breath calms the nervous system.

- **Use movement**—shake out your limbs, take a short walk, dance for a minute. Shake the cobwebs loose.
- **Try simple bodywork**—foam rolling, massage, trigger-point pressure—to release stuck emotional energy.

Flow is a release.

Letting go physically tells your brain:

"It's safe now. You can create."

HOW TO INVITE FLOW: BUILDING THE CONDITIONS FOR MAGIC

Flow may seem elusive, but you can make it easier to enter by creating the right environment around you—and within you.

- **Set Clear Goals — But Leave Space for Surprise**

    Know your "what," but stay open to how it unfolds. Clarity gives direction, flexibility gives magic.

- **Find Your Edge**

    Flow thrives at the balance between challenge and skill. Stretch slightly past your comfort zone, but not so far you snap.

- **Craft a Sacred Space**

    Flow resists chaos. Create environments that feel focused, clear, and inspiring. Music, lighting, scents—all of it matters.

- **Use Rituals to Signal Flow**

    Light a candle. Put on a favorite playlist. Do three deep breaths. Rituals tell your mind: "It's time."

- **Time-Block Deep Work Sessions**

    Protect pockets of uninterrupted focus. Even 90 minutes of pure presence can transform your output.

- **Celebrate Tiny Wins**

    Every small moment of momentum matters. Acknowledge it. Let progress energize you instead of waiting for huge milestones.

- **Engage in What You Love**

    When you enjoy the task itself, flow doesn't need to be forced. It shows up naturally.

FINAL THOUGHT:

You don't have to fight your way into flow.

You have to **clear the noise**, **relax the grip**, and **trust the moment**.

When your body is open, your mind is clear, and your heart is engaged—flow becomes not only possible, but inevitable.

You don't chase flow.

You allow it.

And once you learn how to enter this state, life changes:

Creativity becomes effortless.

Success feels natural.

Joy becomes your baseline.

In the next chapter, **How to Make Affirmations Really Work to Manifest Your Dreams and Desires**, I'll explore how to speak directly to your subconscious—and amplify the flow you've started to unlock.

NOTES

NOTES

NOTES

NOTES

NOTES

NOTES

NOTES

NOTES

NOTES

NOTES

6

HOW TO MAKE AFFIRMATIONS REALLY WORK TO MANIFEST YOUR DREAMS AND DESIRES

Before we dive in, I want to clarify something — especially if you've ever worked with affirmations before.

Maybe you've tried repeating powerful statements — simple, uplifting phrases meant to shift your mindset and energy. And for many people, these affirmations *do* work. They help create focus, clarity, and even transformation — especially when your emotional field is relatively clear and you're not carrying deep inner resistance.

But what I've discovered is this:

There's another group of people — maybe you're one of them — for whom affirmations don't land at all.

They feel empty, even irritating. And no matter how often you repeat them, they don't change how you feel inside.

If that's you, it's not because you're doing something wrong.

It's because you're carrying unresolved emotional weight — guilt, grief, fear, regret — often buried so deeply in your subconscious that it blocks new beliefs from taking hold.

This chapter is for you — the person who has done the work, but still feels stuck. It's not about layering happy words on top of pain. It's about clearing the emotional debris first, so the seeds of affirmation can actually take root and grow.

You can't build a new belief system on top of unresolved wounds.

This chapter shows you how to prepare the soil — and then plant something real.

WHY AFFIRMATIONS SOMETIMES FAIL

At some point in your personal development journey, you've probably heard something like this:

"Just say it enough times and you'll believe it."

"You become what you affirm."

"Your words shape your reality."

While these ideas are popular (and even partly true), what they *don't* address is the internal pushback that happens when your subconscious mind doesn't believe a word you're saying.

You can say "I am worthy" a hundred times.

But if deep down you feel shame or self-loathing… your subconscious will reject it.

Not only will it reject it — it may even double down on the opposite belief.

This is the emotional friction that makes people abandon affirmations altogether. They think they're broken. Or that affirmations are a scam. But the truth is simpler:

You can't affirm over a wound. You have to heal the wound first.

That's why this chapter exists — to help you heal the inner resistance that's blocking your power to rewire your mind and shift your vibration.

MY EXPERIENCE WITH ASKFIRMATIONS

At one point, I explored a trend called "askfirmations" — turning affirmations into questions. Instead of saying "I am wealthy," you ask:

"Why am I so wealthy?"

"Why is everything working out for me?"

"How come I'm so successful?"

It sounded clever. It was gaining popularity. So I tried it.

But instead of motivating me, it triggered me.

Those questions didn't feel empowering — they felt like lies. They made me hyper-aware of the gap between where I was and where I wanted to be. Instead of attracting abundance, I was attracting frustration.

I wasn't alone. Many people I spoke to had the same experience. These affirmations clashed with their emotional reality — and instead of soothing their subconscious, they irritated it.

That's when I realized something critical:

Affirmations only work when they feel emotionally possible.

They don't need to feel 100% true. They just need to feel *within reach*.

You don't need to believe the whole statement — but you need to be open to the idea that it *could* be true.

WHY DENIAL DOESN'T WORK

One of the biggest blocks to making affirmations work is **emotional denial**.

In personal growth circles, there's often pressure to be "high-vibe" — to always stay positive, speak light, and avoid anything that sounds "negative."

So what do people do?

They bury their real feelings under a pile of nice-sounding mantras.

They say "I am grateful and blessed" while suppressing pain.

They say "Everything is working out" while quietly falling apart.

Here's the truth:

What you don't face, you can't shift.

What you suppress, you subconsciously attract.

You have to **acknowledge the pain first.** That's not weakness — that's healing. And once you've acknowledged it, welcomed it, and begun releasing it… *then* your affirmations have a place to land.

THE GROUNDWORK: FEEL IT FIRST

Before you can reprogram your subconscious with empowering affirmations, you must open the emotional space for them to be received.

Here's how:

1. Acknowledge What You're Feeling

Be radically honest. No sugarcoating.

Say:

"I feel stuck."

"I feel scared."

"I feel like I don't deserve more."

Admit it. Let it breathe.

2. Welcome the Feeling Instead of Fighting It

Say internally:

"This belongs here. I don't need to fix it. I just need to feel it."

Let your nervous system soften. Let your body exhale.

3. Release It Through Breath, Touch, or Movement

- Use **breathwork** (slow belly breaths) while saying:

"I release and let go."

- Try **TFT tapping** or the **Sedona Method**
- Gently stretch or massage tense areas where emotions live in the body
- This opens the way for new energy to enter.

Only after that process… do we affirm.

CRAFTING AFFIRMATIONS THAT WORK

Now that the ground is clear, you can build affirmations that feel nourishing instead of fake.

Use Broad, Open Language

"I am open to abundance."

"I welcome clarity."

"I trust something new is unfolding."

Anchor to Emotions, Not Outcomes

"I love feeling financially free."

"I enjoy the calm of being supported."

"It feels safe to trust."

Make It Feel Real

Use this template:

"I am grateful for [desired experience] because it makes me feel [emotion]."

Examples:

"I am grateful for new opportunities because they make me feel inspired."

"I am grateful for peace in my body because it makes me feel safe."

THE 21-DAY AFFIRMATION CHALLENGE

Affirmations are like weights for your subconscious. The more consistently you lift, the stronger your beliefs become.

Here's the process:

Morning Practice:

- Write 3 affirmations using the emotional template above
- Say them out loud with feeling

- Look into your eyes in the mirror — connect with your future self

Evening Reflection:

- Journal 1 moment from your day that aligned with any affirmation
- No moment is too small. The shift happens in micro-wins

Nighttime Energy Cleanse: The Bless + Gratitude Prayer

Before bed, try this:

1. Bless those you love — and those you resent.

"I bless [name]. I release them. I allow peace between us."

2. Name what you're grateful for.

"Thank you for this bed. This breath. This new beginning."

This softens your heart and clears your field overnight.

DAILY AFFIRMATION FOR EMOTIONAL TRUTH

> *"I speak words that honor my pain, my healing, and my power.*
>
> *I am safe to feel.*
>
> *I am ready to rise."*

THE TRUTH

You don't have to lie to yourself to create change.

You just have to tell the truth — and then lovingly speak what you're *open* to becoming.

That's the difference between toxic positivity and empowered manifestation.

And when your affirmations rise from that place of honesty?

They're not just words — they become reality.

In the next chapter, *Taking Action Without Attachment*, I'll explore how to move with purpose while letting go of obsession. You'll learn how surrendering control over results is often the very key that makes them appear.

NOTES

NOTES

NOTES

NOTES

NOTES

NOTES

NOTES

NOTES

NOTES

NOTES

7

TAKING ACTION WITHOUT ATTACHMENT

Modern society worships the hustle—the constant chase for success, validation, and results.

We're told to push harder, move faster, achieve more.

But too often, this mindset leads not to fulfillment, but to burnout, anxiety, and the deep, gnawing feeling that no matter how much we do, it's never enough.

What if real power doesn't come from controlling outcomes—but from trusting the process?

This chapter is about learning how to take bold, meaningful action—**without gripping so tightly** to what happens next.

It's about discovering the freedom that comes when you give your best without letting your worth ride on the result.

BALANCING EFFORT AND DETACHMENT

Action is necessary. Goals matter.

But **attachment**—the desperate clinging to specific outcomes—traps us.

When we over-focus on "how" and "when" things must unfold, we often block the very flow we're trying to create.

We choke creativity, we tighten emotionally, and we lose connection to the deeper wisdom guiding our steps.

Detachment doesn't mean giving up.

It means showing up fully—then releasing the need to control the result.

Imagine climbing a mountain:

If all you care about is reaching the summit, every step becomes a burden.

But if you find joy in the climb—the fresh air, the strength building in your legs, the lessons in every obstacle—you win no matter how high you reach.

This shift—from outcome obsession to present-moment engagement—is where fulfillment begins.

Effort is yours.

Outcome is not.

HOW ATTACHMENT SHOWS UP (AND HOW IT BLOCKS YOU)

You know you're attached when:

- Your happiness depends entirely on external success.
- You measure yourself by results, not by growth or courage.
- You push and push, even when life is signaling you to pause, pivot, or trust.

Attachment creates anxiety, desperation, rigidity.

It whispers: *"If this doesn't happen exactly how I want, it means I failed."*

But life rarely unfolds exactly how we script it.

Attachment narrows possibilities.

Detachment **expands them**.

When you release the grip, you create space for outcomes better than you imagined.

REAL TOOLS FOR TAKING ACTION WITHOUT ATTACHMENT

Here's how to **live the mindset of detached action** in practical ways:

- **Set Clear Intentions, Not Rigid Expectations**

    Define what you want. Visualize success.

    Then stay open to how and when it unfolds—knowing life often has better timing than you do.

- **Focus on the Work, Not the Applause**

    Love the act itself—writing, building, creating, serving.

    The joy is in the doing, not just in the recognition.

- **Embrace Feedback Without Losing Yourself**

    When you act unattached, feedback becomes information—not a referendum on your worth.

- **Let Failure Be a Door, Not a Wall**

    When things don't go your way, don't tighten your grip—loosen it.

    See the detour. Stay fluid. Trust the long game.

- **Breathe Through the Unknown**

    Instead of tensing up when outcomes wobble, pause. Breathe.

Remind yourself: *"I am doing my part. The rest is unfolding beyond me."*

MICRO-EXERCISE: THE "BEST EFFORT, LOOSE GRIP" PRACTICE

Before you start a major action—writing an email, having a difficult conversation, launching a project—pause and ask:

- Have I clarified my intention?
- Am I willing to give my full heart to this?
- Am I willing to trust the timing, even if it's different than I imagined?

If you can answer **yes** to all three—you are ready to move forward with purpose, but without chains.

REAL-WORLD EXAMPLE: THE ARTIST WHO LET GO

Years ago, I spoke with a musician who had been rejected by major record labels for years.

Frustrated and burned out, he decided to stop chasing deals. Instead, he focused entirely on creating the best music he could—for himself, not for approval.

Within a year, he independently released an album that caught the attention of millions—without trying to control or predict the outcome.

What changed?

He stayed in action.

But he released attachment.

And in doing so, he moved into alignment with flow.

THE POWER OF GENTLE PERSISTENCE

Taking action without attachment doesn't mean you only act once and walk away.

It means you keep showing up—with heart, with commitment—but **without gripping** the timeline or the outcome.

It's persistence infused with trust, not desperation.

Think of a river carving through rock.

It doesn't rage or demand.

It simply flows—with steady power—trusting that persistence itself shapes destiny.

REFLECTION QUESTIONS

- Where in your life are you pushing too hard, trying to force an outcome?
- What action could you take today if you trusted that your worth isn't tied to success or failure?
- How would it feel to move forward freely, without clinging to results?

DAILY AFFIRMATION FOR DETACHED ACTION

"I move forward with full heart and open hands.

I trust the journey.

I surrender the outcome.

I am free."

FINAL THOUGHT:

Taking action is noble.

Dreaming is courageous.

Building, striving, reaching—they're all beautiful.

TAKING ACTION WITHOUT ATTACHMENT

But the most powerful move you can make is to act boldly—**without making your joy, your identity, or your peace depend on the outcome.**

Move with purpose.

Release with trust.

And let life meet you halfway in ways you never expected.

NOTES

NOTES

NOTES

NOTES

NOTES

NOTES

NOTES

NOTES

NOTES

NOTES

CONCLUSION AND A CALL TO ACTION

In a world that often equates success with control and certainty, surrender can feel counterintuitive.

Yet, as you've explored throughout this book, true strength, clarity, and even miracles often arise the moment we let go.

Surrender isn't about giving up.

It's about stepping into a new way of living—one marked by trust, flexibility, and peace.

THE POWER OF SURRENDER IN REAL LIFE

I want to share a few moments that show how real—and transformative—surrender can be.

One story that sticks with me is about a woman who spent months trying to land her dream job.

She networked tirelessly, tweaked her resume endlessly, and applied for every opportunity she could find.

CONCLUSION AND A CALL TO ACTION

When nothing worked, she took a pause—not to give up, but to step back and reset.

She asked herself: "What if I trusted that the right opportunity would come—not through constant pushing, but through alignment?"

So she shifted her energy.

Instead of obsessing over results, she began focusing on enjoying her current work, reconnecting with what she loved about her field, and caring for herself.

Within a month, she got a call—completely unexpected—from a company she hadn't even applied to.

A friend had recommended her, and the job turned out to be better than anything she had chased after.

By letting go, she opened the door to something better than she ever expected.

Another example is a man who dreamed of writing a book.

For years, he started and stopped, paralyzed by fear of failure.

Finally, he surrendered his need for perfection—and gave himself permission to simply write badly if he had to.

Once he let go of the pressure, the words flowed.

He finished the draft in 90 days, something he had been struggling to do for five years.

Surrender doesn't mean doing nothing.

It means doing your part—and trusting life to meet you halfway.

When you loosen your grip on how things "must" happen, you invite new possibilities.

You create space for flow, ease, and even miracles.

EMBRACING THE UNCERTAINTY

Life will always contain unknowns.

The more we try to control every detail, the more we limit ourselves to only what we can foresee—and shut out all the surprises life could offer.

Surrender is about softening your grip on expectations and allowing life to unfold, sometimes in ways more beautiful than anything you could have planned.

This doesn't mean abandoning your goals.

It means trusting there's more than one right path.

When you embrace uncertainty, you allow yourself to be surprised by joy.

You discover strengths you didn't know you had.

You forge deeper connections.

You become more resilient with each step forward.

LIVING A LIFE OF TRUST AND OPENNESS

True surrender is rooted in trust—trust in yourself, trust in life, and trust in something greater than your immediate understanding.

It's believing that even when the path looks unclear, you're still being guided.

Living with trust doesn't erase challenges.

It makes them easier to navigate.

It transforms obstacles into lessons, misdirections into useful detours, and failures into doorways.

The more you live this way, the more life begins to feel not like a battle to win—but like a dance to experience.

A CALL TO ACTION: THE 30-DAY SURRENDER CHALLENGE

Reading about surrender is one thing.

Living it is another.

If you're ready to experience what surrender can unlock for you, I invite you to begin a personal experiment:

The 30-Day Surrender Challenge

For the next 30 days, consciously practice letting go of control in at least one small way each day.

It might be:

- Trusting a loved one to handle something without micromanaging.
- Trusting yourself to speak with presence instead of second-guessing every word.
- Releasing attachment to the outcome of a project at work.

Each day, take 3–5 minutes to journal:

- What did I surrender today?
- How did it feel in the moment?
- What did I notice afterward?

By the end of 30 days, you'll have a living record of your relationship with trust, openness, and flow—and you may find that life responds more kindly and creatively when you stop trying to force it.

FINAL THOUGHT

This is your moment.

Take a deep breath.

Loosen your grip.

Step into a new way of living—one marked not by frantic control, but by steady trust.

The journey of surrender isn't always easy.

But it's real, raw, and deeply rewarding.

And it begins now—with one choice:

To trust yourself.

To trust life.

And to let go.

APPENDIX:

PRACTICAL TOOLS FOR LETTING GO

TOOLS & TECHNIQUES FOR THE PRACTICE OF SURRENDER

Letting go isn't just a mindset — it's a practice. It's something you do with your mind, body, and heart. And like any skill, it gets easier the more you practice.

In this appendix, you'll find a collection of simple, powerful techniques you can start using today to release tension, emotional baggage, and the need to control. You don't need any prior experience or special training — just a willingness to try and a little time each day.

APPENDIX: PRACTICAL TOOLS FOR LETTING GO

1. TFT
(THOUGHT FIELD THERAPY / TAPPING)

What it is:

A self-healing technique that involves tapping specific points on your face and body while thinking about something that causes emotional stress.

Why it works:

It calms your nervous system and releases emotional charge — like flipping off a switch on anxiety or fear.

How to do it:

1. Think of something that's bothering you (a memory, feeling, or fear).
2. Begin tapping gently with two fingers on the following points, about 5–7 taps each:
   - Side of the hand (karate chop point)
   - Eyebrow (where the brow starts)
   - Side of eye (on the bone)
   - Under the eye (cheekbone)
   - Under nose
   - Chin
   - Collarbone
   - Under the arm

3. While tapping, say out loud:

> *"Even though I feel [insert feeling], I deeply and completely accept myself."*

4. Repeat until you feel a shift or calmness.

- Time: 3–5 minutes
- Tip: You can find many guided tapping videos online for extra support.

2. THE SEDONA METHOD

What it is:

A simple technique to help you release any unwanted emotion by asking yourself three key questions.

Why it works:

It doesn't fight your feelings — it welcomes them and lets them dissolve.

How to do it:

When you feel an intense emotion (stress, fear, anger, etc.), sit quietly and ask yourself:

1. **"Could I let this go?"** (Yes/No — don't overthink it)
2. **"Would I let this go?"** (Yes/No)
3. **"When?"** (The only answer that matters: *Now*)

APPENDIX: PRACTICAL TOOLS FOR LETTING GO

Repeat the three questions several times, even if the answers are "no." The act of asking begins the release.

- Time: 2–10 minutes
- Tip: Use this anytime during your day — even while walking or sitting in traffic.

3. BREATH RELEASE TECHNIQUE

What it is:

A short breathing practice that helps calm your nervous system and let go of stuck emotion.

Why it works:

Your breath is directly connected to your emotional state. Shallow breath = tension. Deep breath = release.

How to do it:

1. Sit or lie down comfortably.
2. Place one hand on your chest and the other on your lower belly.
3. Inhale through your nose for 4 seconds, letting your belly rise.
4. Hold your breath for 4 seconds.
5. Exhale slowly through your mouth for 6–8 seconds, whispering:

"I release and let go."

6. Repeat 5–10 rounds.

   - Time: 5 minutes
   - Tip: You can use this right before bed, before a difficult conversation, or anytime you feel overwhelmed.

4. PRAYER & BLESSING RITUAL (NIGHT PRACTICE)

What it is:

A peaceful nighttime routine to release emotional heaviness and shift into gratitude before sleep.

Why it works:

What you focus on before sleep sets the tone for your emotional state — and even your dreams.

How to do it: Before bed, close your eyes and whisper or think through these two steps:

Step 1: Bless everyone — especially those who've hurt you.

"I bless [insert name]. I forgive them. I release this burden."

Step 2: Give thanks for what you have.

> *"Thank you for my bed, my health, this quiet moment, the lessons of today."*

Let this ritual close your day with grace and clear your emotional field overnight.

- Time: 3–5 minutes
- Tip: Keep a small journal by your bed to jot down one blessing and one gratitude each night.

5. TRIGGER-POINT PHYSICAL RELEASE

What it is:

A body-based technique that helps release emotions trapped in your muscles through touch or movement.

Why it works:

Your body stores old pain — and sometimes, a simple massage or stretch can unlock years of tension.

How to do it:

- Lie down and scan your body for tension.
- Press gently into tight spots (shoulders, hips, jaw, lower back).
- Breathe deeply into the tension.
- Let any thoughts, memories, or emotions rise — don't judge them. Just feel.
- As you exhale, say:

"I let this go."

You can also use tools like foam rollers or massage balls to apply pressure gently.

- Time: 5–10 minutes
- Tip: If a strong emotion surfaces, pause, breathe, and stay present. Let the body guide the release.

6. NIGHTLY REFLECTION FORMAT

What it is:

A journaling method to track emotional shifts and build emotional clarity over time.

Why it works:

Writing makes your internal world visible. It shows you patterns, progress, and where you still need to let go.

How to do it (every evening):

1. **What did I hold on to today?**
2. (A frustration, disappointment, fear, or tension.)
3. **What am I ready to release?**
4. (Be honest — one emotion, thought, or pattern.)
5. **What did I do well?**
6. (Even something small. Acknowledge yourself.)
7. **What am I grateful for right now?**
8. (End with appreciation. This anchors peace.)

- Time: 5–10 minutes
- Tip: This is not about perfection. It's about noticing. Keep it simple and honest.

FINAL THOUGHTS

These tools don't require hours of meditation, expensive programs, or spiritual mastery. They just require your presence. Your willingness. Your decision to **let go a little more each day**.

You don't need to be perfect.

You just need to **practice**.

Because the more you practice letting go…

… the more space you create for joy, peace, love, success, and clarity to enter your life — naturally, without force.

This is the art of surrender.

NOTES

APPENDIX: PRACTICAL TOOLS FOR LETTING GO

NOTES

APPENDIX: PRACTICAL TOOLS FOR LETTING GO

NOTES

NOTES

APPENDIX: PRACTICAL TOOLS FOR LETTING GO

NOTES

APPENDIX: PRACTICAL TOOLS FOR LETTING GO

NOTES

APPENDIX: PRACTICAL TOOLS FOR LETTING GO

NOTES

APPENDIX: PRACTICAL TOOLS FOR LETTING GO

NOTES

APPENDIX: PRACTICAL TOOLS FOR LETTING GO

NOTES

APPENDIX: PRACTICAL TOOLS FOR LETTING GO

NOTES

APPENDIX: PRACTICAL TOOLS FOR LETTING GO

NOTES

APPENDIX: PRACTICAL TOOLS FOR LETTING GO

NOTES

APPENDIX: PRACTICAL TOOLS FOR LETTING GO

NOTES

APPENDIX: PRACTICAL TOOLS FOR LETTING GO

NOTES

APPENDIX: PRACTICAL TOOLS FOR LETTING GO

NOTES

NOTES

NOTES

APPENDIX: PRACTICAL TOOLS FOR LETTING GO

NOTES

APPENDIX: PRACTICAL TOOLS FOR LETTING GO

NOTES

APPENDIX: PRACTICAL TOOLS FOR LETTING GO

NOTES

APPENDIX: PRACTICAL TOOLS FOR LETTING GO

NOTES

APPENDIX: PRACTICAL TOOLS FOR LETTING GO

NOTES

APPENDIX: PRACTICAL TOOLS FOR LETTING GO

NOTES

APPENDIX: PRACTICAL TOOLS FOR LETTING GO

NOTES

APPENDIX: PRACTICAL TOOLS FOR LETTING GO

NOTES

APPENDIX: PRACTICAL TOOLS FOR LETTING GO

NOTES

APPENDIX: PRACTICAL TOOLS FOR LETTING GO

NOTES

APPENDIX: PRACTICAL TOOLS FOR LETTING GO

NOTES

NOTES

APPENDIX: PRACTICAL TOOLS FOR LETTING GO

NOTES

NOTES

APPENDIX: PRACTICAL TOOLS FOR LETTING GO

NOTES

APPENDIX: PRACTICAL TOOLS FOR LETTING GO

NOTES

APPENDIX: PRACTICAL TOOLS FOR LETTING GO

NOTES

APPENDIX: PRACTICAL TOOLS FOR LETTING GO

NOTES

APPENDIX: PRACTICAL TOOLS FOR LETTING GO

NOTES

APPENDIX: PRACTICAL TOOLS FOR LETTING GO

NOTES

APPENDIX: PRACTICAL TOOLS FOR LETTING GO

NOTES

APPENDIX: PRACTICAL TOOLS FOR LETTING GO

NOTES

NOTES

APPENDIX: PRACTICAL TOOLS FOR LETTING GO

NOTES

NOTES

APPENDIX: PRACTICAL TOOLS FOR LETTING GO

NOTES

APPENDIX: PRACTICAL TOOLS FOR LETTING GO

NOTES

APPENDIX: PRACTICAL TOOLS FOR LETTING GO

NOTES

APPENDIX: PRACTICAL TOOLS FOR LETTING GO

NOTES

APPENDIX: PRACTICAL TOOLS FOR LETTING GO

NOTES

APPENDIX: PRACTICAL TOOLS FOR LETTING GO

NOTES

ACKNOWLEDGMENTS

First and foremost, my heartfelt thanks go to *Rocco*. Your insights helped refine the heart of this book. You pushed me to go deeper, add richer stories, and bring out the emotional layers that now make this work truly resonate with readers. I'm immensely grateful for your support and perspective.

To *Dimitry*, thank you for your incredible feedback. Your attention to detail and thoughtful suggestions gave the book its final polish. Your contribution ensured it was not only ready to be released, but ready to make an impact. I deeply value the role you played in shaping its final form.

A special thanks to *Isa*, whose design work brought the interior of this book to life. It's always a joy to see how you transform words into beautiful, intuitive layouts that enhance the reading experience. Your creative eye elevated every page.

Lastly, I'm deeply thankful to *Mercy*, the talent behind the book's cover design. As the saying goes, people judge a book by its cover—and thanks to you, I know they'll be judging it well. Your work gave the book its most visible and lasting impression.

To all of you — thank you for helping bring *The Art of Surrender* into the world with clarity, beauty, and heart.

ABOUT THE AUTHOR

Simon Bedros is on a personal and professional mission to empower ambitious individuals to create extraordinary success by mastering strategic vision, cultivating resilience, and harnessing the transformative power of surrender.

With extensive experience advising thousands of businesses worldwide—from dynamic startups and mid-sized enterprises to Fortune 500 corporations—Simon has established himself as a leading voice in sales psychology, strategic marketing, and crisis management. Industry leaders including Google, Visa, Salesforce, Oracle, and MetLife have turned to Simon for his unparalleled ability to turn challenges into growth opportunities, leveraging both traditional strategies and cutting-edge AI-driven technologies.

Simon discovered his passion for transformative leadership through nearly a decade of high-impact roles, developing a profound understanding of how mindset and strategic insight shape business success. As the Founder of Simon Bedros Consulting Group and CEO of AI Sales Coach, he uniquely blends human psychology and advanced technology to set new standards in sales and business coaching.

ABOUT THE AUTHOR

His bestselling book, *The Perfect Closing Script*, has sold over 100,000 copies globally, solidifying his reputation as a transformative thought leader. Building upon this success, Simon's latest book, *The Art of Surrender: How Letting Go Attracts What You Truly Desire*, guides readers through the powerful paradox of releasing emotional barriers to unlock unprecedented levels of success and fulfillment.

Outside of his professional endeavors, Simon is a passionate speaker, regularly sharing actionable insights at international conferences and industry events. He cherishes exploring innovative business concepts and, most importantly, spending quality time with his family and friends.

Connect with Simon on LinkedIn to gain deeper insights, access transformative strategies, and join a community dedicated to growth, resilience, and extraordinary achievement